Published by Lang Books
A Division of R.A. Lang Card Co., Ltd.
514 Wells Street
Delafield, WI 53018

10 9 8 7 6 5 4 3 2 1

ISBN No. 0-7413-0437-1

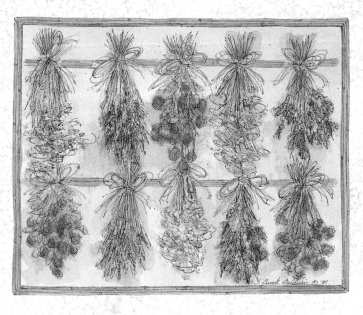

Presented with love
to
Cindy
from
Bob
on this day
October 3, 2001
18 wonderful months of
our new friendship and
Love !!

To my daughters, Julie, Sara, and Carrie.
I feel thrice blessed to be the mother of
three such delightful and accomplished
young women.
AMR

To Katie Grace,
my daughter, my joy ♡
SBB

en Sherri and I were discussing the title for this mother to daughter book, we both thought about the tendency of little girls to pick their mothers bouquets of wildflowers. And even though the bouquets they pick are often made up of more weeds than flowers, we mothers always lovingly put them in a vase because to us, those little bouquets symbolize the purest form of love - they are quite literally "bouquets of love" from daughter to mother.

Thus, we decided that this book should be a gift in kind from mother to daughter - a collection of loving advice which is our own special version of a "bouquet of love."

the Bee's Knees

J. Buck Baldwin ©1999

Sustaining Personal Growth

Thyme

Thymus vulgaris

As the mother of three grown daughters,
I can truly say that mothers and daughters have
a special bond that is deeply rooted.
A mother who is blessed with the opportunity of
raising a daughter plants the seeds of wisdom,
watches as her daughter grows and matures,
and then observes lovingly
as her daughter blooms into womanhood.

Some of us are like wheelbarrows —
only useful when pushed, and very easily upset.
~Jack Herbert~

The only way to sustain meaningful
personal growth is to avoid being
like a wheelbarrow.
Always push yourself,
and then don't get upset
when you have a setback!

If you wait until exactly
the right time to do
something, you will never
begin. So just go out
there every day and do
what you have to do!
Begin now.

*E*ach person needs a challenge - running, painting, swimming, gardening. The activity itself is less important than the act of drawing on your own resources and growing from the experience.

Children love to plant a bean
and watch the sprout grow and mature;
this experience teaches them several lessons:
patience while waiting for the bean to sprout,
wonder at the life peaking up out of the dirt,
and joy when the bean turns into a real plant.
Patience, wonder, and joy -
not a bad yield for one little bean!

chamomile · peppermint · tea · orange pekoe · cinnamon

English breakfast · apple

comfrey · Earl Grey

Adapting

to

Change

Steel Magnolias

Remember the movie? I know some true-to-life steel magnolias who have been friends since grammar school. They were newly married and then young mothers together; they have experienced the joy of both graduations and marriages, as well as the pain of the death of a child. Now that their husbands are gone, they are still friends and living life to the hilt every day - seeing plays, going on cruises, growing flowers, attending church. These steel magnolias are the epitome of adaptability.

*H*ow can something called a weed
possibly be associated with the graceful
butterfly? Butterfly weeds are actually cheerful
bright orange clumps of flowers that attract
monarch and swallowtail butterflies. They grow wild,
don't need much water, and are easily transplanted.
This one little "weed" teaches us that
natural beauty attracts beauty.

Butterfly Weed

Everything that grows holds in perfection but a little moment. ~ Shakespeare ~

The morning glory opens in the morning,
and closes by mid-afternoon, lasting but one
day. As you pass through daily life,
remember that many things you see
during the course of a day
won't be there tomorrow -
they are as beautiful and transitory
as the morning glory.

From the withered tree, a flower blooms.
-Zen Saying-

I'm not sure if everything happens for a reason,
but I am sure we can find reason
in everything that happens.
Don't give up - it's always possible
for a beautiful flower to bloom
from the most desolate landscape.

When one door of happiness closes, another opens;
but often we look so long at the closed door that we do not see
the one which has opened for us.
~Helen Keller~

*O*ne of the hardest lessons in life
is learning when to move on.
We often miss wonderful opportunities for
growth and change
because we are so wrapped up in the past.
If it's over and done with, move on!

Traveling across the country has taught me that plants are marvelously adaptable. No matter where you go - deserts, plains, mountains, meadows - plants are able to grow and thrive there. Take a lesson from plants - no matter what the conditions, you can adapt!

Cultivating Happiness

When I see a
row of sunflowers,
I like to think of
them as bright,
happy children,
good-naturedly
holding their faces
up to the sun.
Always look at
the sunshine and
shadows will
soon disappear.

The optimist sees the rose and not its thorns;
the pessimist stares at the thorns, oblivious to the rose.
-Kahlil Gibran-

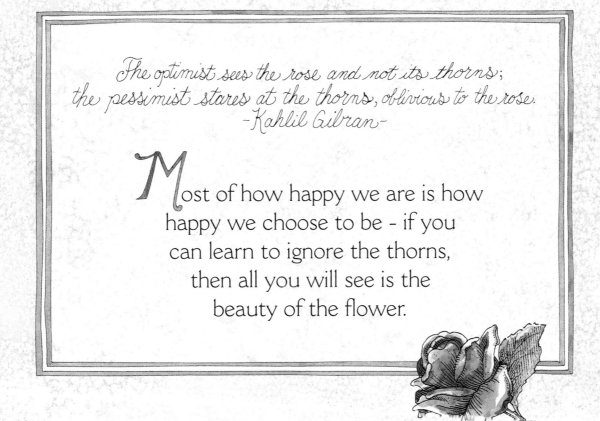

Most of how happy we are is how
happy we choose to be - if you
can learn to ignore the thorns,
then all you will see is the
beauty of the flower.

Sunshine is delicious, rain is refreshing, wind braces up, snow is exhilarating; there is no such thing as bad weather, only different kinds of good weather.
~John Ruskin~

Develop the ability to look at each of life's happenings as a different version of good.

Tending
to
Friends and Family

Daisy Chains

I spent long summer evenings as a little girl,
sitting on the lawn with my cousins, weaving chains of
wildflowers. We called these creations "daisy chains" and
wore them as crowns, necklaces, and bracelets. Those
long evenings taught me the value of time spent with
family and friends, weaving dreams for the future.

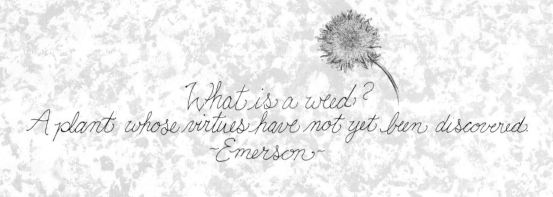

What is a weed?
A plant whose virtues have not yet been discovered.
~Emerson~

The bouquets little girls
pick for their mothers are often
collections of dandelions, chigger weed,
or other random weeds. However, the
value in these little bouquets is the
flowers that make them up; it is the
love that goes into the gift.
True gifts are those given
from a loving heart.

It's no secret to those around me that I have yearned for a sister my entire life. Fortunately, I have found several "sisters" throughout the years and have discovered through them that a true friendship can endure calm or stormy weather and is well worth cultivating. Take care of your "sister relationships".

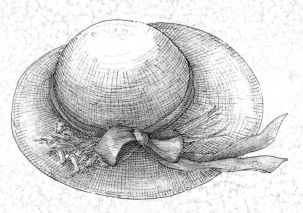

For there is no friend like a sister
In calm or stormy weather.
~Christina Rossetti~

Family Stories

In my family, as in most families,
there are stories that have been passed
down from generation to generation
from mother to daughter.
These stories make up the warp and fabric
of our lives,
they are how we gain our identity,
they tell us where we have been
and where we are going.
Listen to your family stories carefully.

Perennials
and
Annuals

*P*erennials come back year after year,
while shorter-lived annuals provide a bright
splash of color to fill in between growing seasons.
Thus, both are necessary elements of a beautiful
garden. Cultivate a "garden" of friends of both
annuals and perennials - some to provide a bright
splash of color and others to be there year after year,
providing comfort and support. Having all types of
friends will add balance to your life!

The family is one of nature's masterpieces.
~George Santayana~

A family comes in many forms - wherever there are people working together to strengthen, comfort, and sustain each other, they can be rightfully called a family. Make yourself a part of a family no matter where you are.

Planting Seeds

of

Kindness

Lilacs make me smile. My grandmother had a full
hedge of them which bloomed
profusely every spring. Because she loved
lilacs and wanted to share their beauty, she
would often surprise a friend or neighbor by
leaving a huge fragrant bouquet of them
in a mason jar on their doorstep. She
taught me, more than anyone, how little
effort it takes to spread joy and happiness.
Give a gift today of something you love!

I always prefer to believe the best of everybody—
it saves so much trouble.
—Rudyard Kipling—

It's often hard to give other people the
benefit of the doubt, especially when we feel
they are being rude or inconsiderate;
but it saves so much effort to hold tight to
the simple belief that most people are only
doing their best.

As I watch the birds out in our backyard,
I notice that they often fight over the
bird feeder, even though there is plenty of
birdseed to go around. More often than not,
they spill half the seed on the ground during
their little bird scuffles. Some battles just
aren't worth the trouble - in other words,
make sure what you are fighting so hard
for will end up being more than
just "chickenfeed".

Do at least one thing every day for someone else for which you expect no praise, personal gain, or reward. You will be surprised at how much joy this practice can add to your life.

The true meaning of life is to plant trees, under whose shade you do not expect to sit.
—Nelson Henderson—

Gratitude is the fairest
blossom which springs
from the soul.
-Henry Ward Beecher-

As you go through life, there will be many
people - teachers, strangers,
distant relatives, co-workers -
who are kind to you for no particular reason.
When you are able to do so,
be sure to show your gratitude by
repaying "in kind" these
random acts of kindness.

Growing any kind of flower or vegetable teaches us that there is a time in a tender young plant's life when it is weak and vulnerable to outside forces. Keep in mind that people too have "tender moments" in their lives when they need extra care and consideration.

Nurturing Individuality

Children in a family are like flowers in a bouquet:
there's always one determined to face in an opposite direction
from the way the arranger desires.
~Marcelene Cox~

$\mathcal{E}$mbrace individualism -
variety is what makes life interesting.

My cousin, who I visited quite often when I was growing up, lived on a farm. One day we dressed a couple of chickens up in doll clothes and tried to wheel them around in an old baby buggy. If you know anything about chickens, you know they don't take well to fussy clothing and doll buggies. We learned that it never works to try to make something (or someone) into something else. Instead, you just have to accept them for what they are.

After all,
a chicken
can only be
a chicken.

Heather thrives in wide open windy moors
and enjoys living undisturbed
and so has become
the symbol of solitude.
Like this lovely plant,
only in solitude can you think,
evaluate your life,
and grow.

Fostering
Success

In flower gardening, as in any artistic endeavor,
a focal point is anything that draws your
eye and holds it. One of the keys to success is
to have a focal point in your life - that is, some tangible
end that you have in your mind's eye to work towards
achieving every single day.

Instead of waiting
for someone
to bring you
flowers,
go out and grow
your own
garden.

$\mathcal{S}$uccessful gardening involves much
planning, preparation and attention.
Success in life is much the same:
laying a strong foundation,
setting thoughtful goals,
and then giving constant care
and attention to the outcome are all
equally important.

Buck Baldwin

Developing Spirituality

Man is never closer to God than when he is in a garden.
-anonymous-

As you are driving home from work,
fixing dinner, or running errands,
create a garden in your own mind.
This will put you in touch with God
no matter where you are.

All things
work together
for good
to those
who love God.
-Romans 8:28-

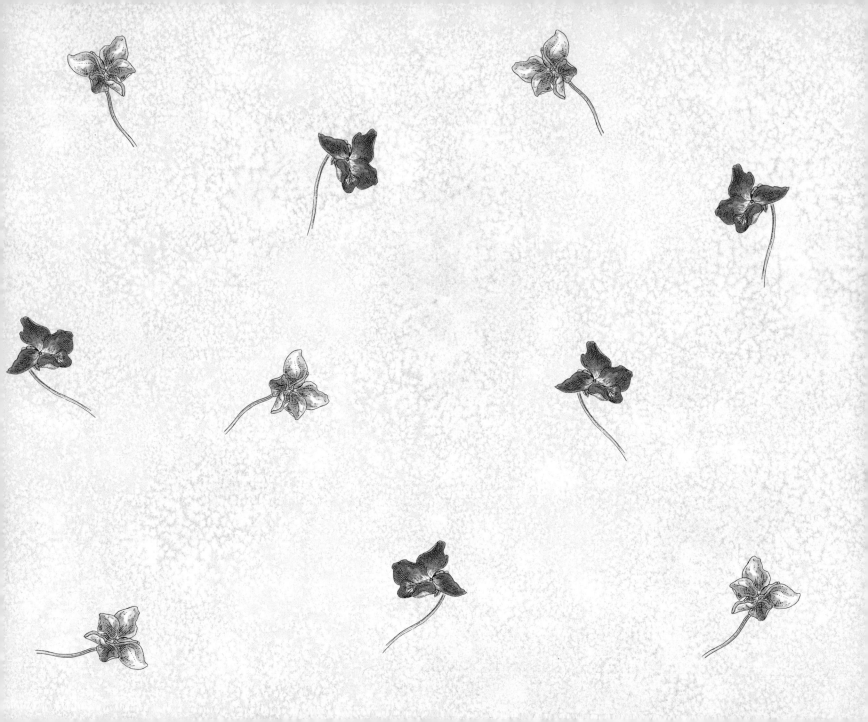